The Holiness of Beauty

JOHN F. BUTLER

———— ★ ————

The Holiness of Beauty

WIPF & STOCK · Eugene, Oregon

Wipf and Stock Publishers
199 W 8th Ave, Suite 3
Eugene, OR 97401

The Holiness of Beauty
By Butler, John F.
Copyright©1961 Methodist Publishing - Epworth Press
ISBN 13: 978-1-4982-0491-0
Publication date 9/10/2014
Previously published by Epworth Press, 1961

Contents

Foreword

THIS BOOKLET has been written at the request of the Society of Christian Artists, a body recently formed to promote the study and practice of Christian art, especially within the Methodist Church. I am grateful for helpful suggestions from two of the Vice-Presidents of the Society, the Rev. Rupert E. Davies, M.A., B.D., and the Rev. Dr. J. Alan Kay. Nevertheless, it is a personal document, and neither the Society nor my advisers are responsible for the views expressed in it. They are my own views in substance, though not completely mine in spirit—for I have had constantly to touch upon great controversies without the possibility of full discussion, often indeed without the possibility of any discussion at all; and thus time and time again brevity has compelled me to excessive dogmatism.

My thanks are due to the Editor of *The Philosophical Quarterly* (Amalner, India) for his kind permission to re-use, in greatly altered form, some material which had appeared in his October 1957 number (XXX.3) in my article entitled 'The Dilemma of Religious Art'.

November 1960   J.F.B.

ONE

Words and Meanings

THIS BOOKLET is an introduction to some of the problems which arise when Churches or individual Christians attempt either to use Christian art or to ignore it. If our discussion is to have any clarity, we must have some definition of 'Christian art', which in turn needs a definition of 'religious art', and this a definition of 'art', and this a definition of 'beauty'. Definitions make a dull beginning; but they can save much floundering later.

I define 'beauty' as 'the quality or value of experiences or objects mediated by sight or hearing which brings joy to the contemplation of a mind trained for its enjoyment'. This definition leans heavily on Aristotle, Aquinas and G. E. Moore, and could be shown to be not so viciously circular as it looks.

Beauty inheres in objects both natural and made by man. In some respects, it would seem to be the same quality in both these types of experience; in other respects, quite distinct: looking at a beautiful woman, and looking at the Venus of Milo, are experiences both akin and different. This odd relationship between natural and manufactured beauty is one of the great problems of aesthetics. Here we shall have to ignore natural beauty; the Church, after all, has very little to do with it. It is true that churches in favoured localities can open their windows to the view, or suit their buildings to some special site; occasionally we hold 'Bluebell Services' or the like; once a year the choir may have to be taken on an outing to the Lakes; physically attractive personnel may bring admirers into a congregation; we always have the critics who say that they find God better in the green fields than inside a stuffy church; Jesus Himself looked on the lilies with a loving eye—and all these facts raise fascinating problems for philosophical thought; but they are not the main problems, and so we pass them by. Here we must concentrate on manufactured beauty, which is art.

More in detail, I take 'art' to be 'the creation, reproduction or reception of manufactured beauty (or the object so created, reproduced or received), this beauty being generally compounded with some other element of purpose, meaning, intuition or emotion, in an organic whole of heightened value'.

That looks very complex; but actually the cumbrous phrases break down naturally into quite simple meanings:

(1) 'Creation, reproduction or reception' reflects the fact that the experience of art is in different kinds for people who have different functional relations to the art. Thus, the painter's experience as he paints his picture, and mine as I look at it, are two distinct kinds of art-experience; the composer's as he writes his music, the pianist's as he plays it, and mine as I listen to it, are three distinct kinds of art-experience. (Further and more subtle distinctions might be drawn; but we will keep things as simple as we can.)

(2) 'Manufactured beauty'—(a) The limitation to manufactured beauty, as distinct from natural, is justified by the fact of the differences between these two types of beauty, already alluded to, and by the fact that, for the most part, the problems and purposes discussed in writings on art apply only to manufactured beauty. (b) So much is this so, that the very inclusion of the word 'beauty' in a definition of art will offend many moderns, who hold that beauty and art have no connection at all, or no necessary connection. This modern doctrine I hold to be a mistake, and ultimately a fatal mistake, though a plausible and in some ways even a helpful one. It is a mistake which has cleared the air of much sentimentality, and has drawn attention to facts which needed remembering, for example, that beauty can reside in unexpected places (in wet tarmac as well as in the 'beauty spot'), and that elements ugly in themselves can be integrated into patterns of artistic beauty, and may even be necessary there, to give tension and passion.

Yet I hold that there must be beauty in a work—beauty in the ordinary sense, as what pleases the trained ear or eye—or the work is not a work of art. Either Picasso's 'Guernica' has some beauty (e.g. of pattern), or it is a mere yell of rage—maybe moral, expressive, important, effective, but not art. It is only at our peril that we cut ourselves off from the Greek urge towards idealizing in art.

(3) The words in brackets, 'or the objects so created, reproduced or received', have been inserted because 'art' is applied, ambiguously, both to experiences and to objects—both to what goes on in minds within studios and art-galleries and to what hangs on the walls there. This width of reference is rarely troublesome, for the context usually restricts it; indeed, it is quite a useful range of meaning, and in any case we cannot here set about any radical reforms of the English language.

(4) The last clause, 'this beauty being generally compounded with some other element . . . in an organic whole of heightened value', has been added to bring into prominence the important fact that art is rarely or never an affair of pure beauty, but is a compound of a peculiar kind, made up of beauty and some other value or values. A picture is not generally a pure pattern in flat colour; it is also a representation. A building is not only a three-dimensional balance of masses and space; it is also a secure and functionally efficient set of rooms. And these elements are not just added together; they are joined and interpenetrated in the peculiar way which G. E. Moore called the making of an 'organic whole'—that is to say, the total quality is other than, and generally greater than, the sum of the qualities of the parts. For example, green is got by adding yellow to blue, but it looks quite different from either of them; and, before actual experience of green, the appearance of green could not have been predicted from experience of yellow or of blue or of both of them. A live cat is compounded of a head, a body and a tail, but it has a quality of existence which you cannot get by taking a cat's head, a cat's body and a cat's tail, and hopefully sticking them together. Likewise (on one theory

of pictorial art) a picture will have a pattern, and thereby possess some value; it may also represent a theme, and thereby possess another kind of value; if these are so combined by the artist as to form a true 'organic whole', then the total value of the picture, as representation-in-pattern, may well be other than, and probably much greater than, the value as pattern and the value as representation simply added together.

(5) 'Purpose, meaning, intuition or emotion' are listed in the definition because they seem to me to be the elements, or at any rate the main elements, which singly or in combination can blend in an organic whole with beauty.

I define 'religion' in the old-fashioned way, as 'man's relationship to God'. By 'God' I mean 'the Ultimate Being, who is also the Perfect Person'.

If we put together these definitions of 'art' and of 'religion', then 'religious art' is defined as 'that art which holds beauty in an organic whole with a religious purpose, meaning or intuition, along with the associated emotions'. Thus, a church is a religious building because it has a religious purpose; a gospel parable is a religious story because it has a religious meaning; a fugue by Bach is a piece of religious music because it mediates religious intuitions; and the church, the parable and the fugue are all religious for the further reason that their religious purpose, meaning or intuition arouses strong associated emotions, which common speech would loosely call 'religious emotions'.

'Christian art' is 'religious art in which the purpose, meaning or intuition involved is Christian'.

It might have been expected that thus to combine Christianity and art would be a direct and simple matter; but history has shown that it is not. Indeed, the very possibility of Christian art is the focus of several difficult problems, to a consideration of which we must now turn. As we do this, I shall concentrate attention on the major visual arts—painting, sculpture and architecture; but where it seems desirable I shall illustrate also from the minor visual arts and from literature and music.

BOOKS RECOMMENDED

Books on art and aesthetics of course are legion: the following paper-backs are both helpful and easily accessible:

Bernhard Berenson: *The Italian Painters of the Renaissance* (Fontana)

Sir Kenneth Clark: *The Nude* (Pelican)

Roger Fry: *Vision and Design* (Pelican)

Eric Newton: *European Painting and Sculpture* (Pelican)

Sir Herbert Read: *Contemporary British Art* and *The Meaning of Art* (Pelican)

I find the following, in solid covers, not too difficult and very helpful in various ways:

E. M. Bartlett: *Types of Aesthetic Judgment*

Clive Bell: *Art*

Ruth Benedict: *Patterns of Culture*

E. F. Carritt: *What is Beauty?*

E. H. Gombrich: *Art and Illusion*

Émile Mâle: *Religious Art from the Twelfth to the Eighteenth Century* (Eng. trans.)

S. E. Rasmussen: *Experiencing Architecture*

Sir Herbert Read: *Art and Society*

I. A. Richards: *Principles of Literary Criticism*

Hans Sedlmayr: *Art in Crisis* (Eng. trans.)

Wladimir Weidlé: *The Dilemma of the Arts* (Eng. trans.)

QUESTIONS FOR DISCUSSION
(1–3 after a visit to a good art gallery):

1. What made the religious pictures there religious?

2. Would you, if you could, have good reproductions of any of them in (*a*) your bedroom, (*b*) your living-room, (*c*) your Sunday school, (*d*) your church? Why, or why not?

3. What did you think the modern artists whose work you saw were 'getting at'?

4. Read (*a*) Matthew 26–28, (*b*) *King Lear*, (*c*) James Elroy Flecker's *Hassan*. What in them is (i) beautiful, (ii) ugly, (iii) great art?

TWO

Why Religion
Cannot Escape Art

THERE IS a popular feeling that art and religion have very little to do with one another. Art, it is supposed, is the concern of long-haired eccentrics on the Left Bank at Paris, who spend their time sipping absinthe in cafés while recuperating from unspeakable orgies in their studios. Contrariwise, religion is a grim business ground out in ugly conventicles by dull people, whose nearest approach to pleasure is the making of their own and other people's lives as drab and colourless as they can. Both these types are caricatures, though with just enough truth in them to sting—and to remind us of how disastrous a thing it may be for both art and religion if they become divorced from one another.

But in fact such divorce is rare; normally art and religion have been very closely associated. Human art began as an instrument for religious magic; that was the purpose of the prehistoric 'Venuses' and cave-paintings. In historic times, the great cultures of the world have been largely built around religious ideas and aspirations. South Indian art is mainly Hindu art; North Indian, Hindu-Muslim art; Ceylonese and Burmese, Buddhist art; mediaeval European, Christian art. It is true, indeed, that even these predominantly religious cultures had their secular aspects (such as Moghul palaces, mediaeval Western castles, and love-lyrics the world over); it is true also that in the Chinese and Roman cultures the secular elements were far more prominent, perhaps even dominant, and that in

Greek culture the religion concerned was so naturalistic that the religious and secular elements in it cannot be sharply distinguished; finally, and most relevantly for our day, it is true that the revival of Greco-Roman traditions at the Renaissance brought about a considerable and increasing secularization of Western art, and that the almost completely secular art which has evolved out of that phase in the West is now sweeping over the rest of the world. Nevertheless, religious art has generally been the greatest and most vital part of the world's cultures, and even yet is an important element in them.

Is that connection a mere accidental fact of history, or can it also be justified as necessary and good? By that I mean, at present, necessary and good for religion; Weidlé and Sedlmayr, in the books referred to above, have shown that it is needful for healthy art, but here I am concerned only with the benefits of the connection for religion. Has religion a need and a duty to seek an alliance with art? There is a very strong case that it has; and I analyse that case into the following seven reasons:

(1) *Religion cannot dispense with art, because it cannot dispense with 'things'.* Maybe a purely individualistic religion would have no cult, and so would need no cult-buildings, cult-objects, cult-music or liturgy, and thus could dispense with all art; but such a religion probably does not exist, and certainly ought not to exist. Every actual religion is in some measure social, and because of this social element has some degree of need of specially religious buildings and other 'things'; and these things, intentionally or not, will be art—good art, bad art, or indifferent art, but still art. Perhaps the Quaker Meeting is the extreme attempt, of any kind that is at all common in modern life, at an art-less form of religion; but even for it a room is needed, and that room is kept scrupulously clean and neat, and the speech in it is sonorous with Biblical cadences. No Christian congregation could well use less art (though many use worse); but art, religious art, is inescapably there. In Islam, the earliest mosques were, of deliberate policy, only reed-fenced courtyards; but were the reeds well-ordered or untidy? Early Methodist services were often, of necessity, plain 'cottage-

meetings'; but were they held in clean rooms or dirty, and what sort of cover did the big Bible have?

(2) *Religious art ranks high in the scale of values.* The consensus of civilized opinion ascribes a great value to art; beauty, artistic beauty, is a very high good. Much of the work of the finest artists and of the most faithful craftsmen has been made for religious purposes or with religious emotions or meanings; surely it is, at the least, none the worse for that. To put the case, temporarily, at its very lowest: Artists love to paint beautiful young women; if a picture of one such is given a blue robe and called 'The Madonna', and thus set in a religious purpose and context (which is exactly the way in which many very fine Renaissance 'Madonnas' were in fact produced), is it a worse picture for that?

Some modern critics, indeed, do maintain that a 'subject' which has major intrinsic significance in itself does actually harm an artist's work, by distracting him from what they take to be his real purposes as an artist. I can myself see no real grounds for such a view, except in so far as it may be taken just as an exaggeration of the needed warning that we must not expect to get great art by the external 'illustration' of great 'subjects'. But there is a large and weighty body of critical opinion today which holds the more moderate view that all subjects are equal to the artist, none being intrinsically 'better' than another. From the religious side, what amounts to the same view is expressed in the frequently-held doctrine that all good art, irrespective of 'subject', is 'sacred art'. The facts of experience, at any rate as they present themselves to me, do not bear these views out; my feelings quite clearly tell me that, granted equal artistic ability and integrity, a major religious subject gives far greater art than any secular subject can. I recall here my definition of religious art as an *organic whole* of art with a religious element, and my claim that organic wholes can have greater value than the sum of the values of their parts. In terms of this outlook, I hold that Bach is of equal musical ability with Mozart (that is to say, supreme), but wrote much greater music, because of the religious purposes and themes in the bulk of his work; and that for like reasons Michelangelo's 'Christ' in S. Maria sopra Minerva is a greater statue than Cellini's 'Perseus', El Greco's 'The Resurrection' in the Prado is a greater painting than Velasquez' 'The Rokeby Venus' in the National Gallery (though that is the quintessence of humanistic beauty), Chartres Cathedral is greater architecture than—well, what secular building can even begin to compare with it?, Arjuna's vision of the Lord in the *Bhagavadgita*, and *The Book of Common Prayer*, are greater poetry than any by Keats, and the last four cantos of Dante's *Paradiso* are the greatest poetry of all.

I am not, of course, suggesting that any dauber's 'Christ' will be better than a great artist's 'Still Life'. It must be realized, too, that 'religious art' has a wider range than might at first appear; *King Lear*, for instance, grapples with cosmic themes and is vibrant with religious energy, even though little of it could be quoted to illustrate points in a theological treatise.

I must also here insist that religious art, if it is to reach the real heights, must hold the religion and the beauty together in a true 'organic whole'. I have already urged that a picture of a handsome young woman in blue labelled 'Madonna' is no worse than an equally competent picture of a handsome young woman in blue not so labelled; but now I must equally urge that it will be no better, if it has nothing religious about it but its label, for it is not yet a religious picture in any sense that gives it added aesthetic value (except adventitiously, by association). It will be no better than the ordinary run of good pictures of young women, unless it has the intention, and succeeds in the intention, of bodying forth the mystery of the Incarnation, in the mingled humility and majesty of the Mother of the God-Man, pondering in her heart the redemptive mysteries which she uniquely serves. Such true fusion of meaning and manner, such thinking and feeling in terms of the medium, such use of the medium simply and solely as the inevitable vehicle of the meaning and feeling—this is a quality which we must pause to consider, because, when it occurs in religious art, it is the basis of the special greatness which belongs to the finest of such art. It is a quality for which it is hard to find a suitable name : Dr. E. M. Bartlett has called it 'sincerity' or 'genuineness'; perhaps this is misleading, since the wholeness in question is in some ways quite different from ordinary, moral, sincerity and integrity. Those are the moral will to avoid discrepancy, conscious or unconscious, between character and utterance : this is the aesthetic technique of avoiding disharmony between matter and medium, and is harder and rarer of achievement. Dr. Bartlett's terminology does indeed bring out the fact of a real and important kinship between the two skills—they are both based on the quest for making expression be adequate to inner meaning. To avoid misunderstandings, then, let us leave this special kind of organic wholeness unnamed, and simply recognize it as the unity, on all levels of the personality, in which a great genius, and he alone, is able fully to bring together intellectual belief, passionate feeling, and mastery of the medium. It is this which is the secret of the highest greatness in art of any kind. In religious art it is, in its fulness, specially hard and specially rare; and it is what gives the very finest religious art the overwhelming value which it alone has among the various forms of art.

Let us illustrate this from religious music. Bach and Haydn were both men of deep personal piety, fully sincere in the ordinary sense; both truly related their piety to their music, preferring religious themes, regarding their music as a divine vocation, and peppering their scores liberally with phrases like 'Ad majorem Dei gloriam', 'To the greater glory of God' (Haydn rather more than Bach); yet as a religious musician Haydn rarely attained to the burning integration of Bach. In the best of Bach's Passion music the religious insight and the music are indissolubly one; but Haydn in his Seven Last Words, though intending to show the agony and the triumph of the Crucifixion as one unified experience in God, yet in fact often lets his music wander off into irrelevant cheerfulness. From this it is but a step to the near-vulgarities of Handel—and then comes the utter collapse of integration and adequacy in Maunder and Stainer. I repeat—this special kind of organic wholeness, in its fulness, is, where religious art is concerned, very hard and very rare. The near-misses, as in Haydn, are works of great genius.

In this and in other ways, a truly religious work of art has a special quality which sets it apart, and sets it very high indeed—very high even when it is not perfect. We must not, indeed, think of this special quality too narrowly, as do some ultra-sensitive critics who deny that Raphael and Bach are fully religious artists because they do not exhibit the same type of spirituality as that in the Byzantine mosaics and Vittoria, but we ought to recognize the fact which these criticisms distort, the fact that (say) Palestrina is a musician on a vastly higher plane than (say) Schumann.

I take it, then, that religious art of many types can be justified as having a very high level indeed in the hierarchy of the cultural values. That view is perhaps unusual, being generally denied altogether by the humanists or distorted by the neo-Byzantines; but it has a very respectable ancestry, being substantially what was maintained through the whole classical tradition, from 'Longinus' to Burke, in the distinction between the 'beautiful' and the 'sublime'.

This stage of the argument must end, unfortunately, on a note of warning. Counterbalancing the cheerful fact that good religious art is one of humanity's high peaks, is the distressing fact that bad religious art is one of humanity's depths. For the power of the 'organic whole' works both ways. Secular sentimentalities, such as those on human sex-love, like the song 'It was a rose, a little, little rose', are just bad art, and nothing much worse than that (one can say if one likes that they trifle improperly with great subjects, but that is at the risk of being over-solemn); but religious sentimentalities like Sankey's really offend—they are cheap trifling with very great things. I could not bring myself to accuse Sankey and his brethren of insincerity in the ordinary sense, not even in the unconscious; but in the artistic sense of the word they are the arch-practitioners of it, and that is why their work hurts.

(3) Besides this intrinsic value as an end-in-itself, *religious*

art also has another kind of value, *instrumental value*, by way of edification and inspiration. Plato and Tolstoy admitted no other value in art but this instrumental one, and Tolstoy admitted even that only on low levels; but the fact that it is erroneous to suppose that art has only instrumental values should not prevent us from recognizing the facts that art in general and religious art in particular *do* have instrumental values, and that these may be important. Religious art 'does the work of an evangelist' on a variety of levels, from merely illustrating simple truths for simple folk to complicated kindlings of high spiritual visions in men of genius. In all kinds of ways Abbot Suger's words on the doors of St.-Denis are true: *'Mens hebes ad verum per materialia surgit'*—'Physical beauty wings the dull mind toward Heaven.' St. Bonaventura listed some of them when he defended the use of religious images: 'because simple souls exist, because our feelings are sluggish, and because our memories fail.'

On a naïve level, the wonder of mediaeval stained glass was created (so we are told, though personally I doubt it) in order that it might be a 'poor man's Bible' for the catechetical benefit of the illiterate masses. Even nowadays, I suspect that a good deal of the Christian semi-belief that persists in pagan England is grounded in dim memories of cathedrals visited during coach-tours. More deeply, the hymns we use, chosen for their sturdy God-filled words and tunes, are not only means by which we express our worship of God, but also means by which God inspires and edifies us: Wesley in his 1779 Preface (reprinted in modern editions of *The Methodist Hymn-Book*) had some peculiar but basically excellent reflections on this. Millions of Christian souls of all levels of culture are nourished daily by truths which come to them in the cadences of the Authorized Version of the Bible, the Missal, the Prayer-Book. I personally remember most vividly how, on the Sunday morning before one close to me died, the wireless played a Bach chorale which I had never heard before, *'Vor deinen Thron tret' ich hiermit'*, the one said to have been dictated by Bach on his death-bed; and I learned from it just what I then sorely needed to know.

21

On a higher level yet, very great souls like Dante, Rembrandt and Blake fought their personal way to their beliefs as they moulded their problems into their art. As Robert Bridges put it:

> *... Art, as it createth new forms of beauty,*
> *awakeneth new ideas that advance the spirit*
> *in the life of Reason to the wisdom of God.*

Much of this awakening is on the conscious level, and could perhaps be done by other agencies than art; but much of it is done in the unconscious, maybe even on the level of a racial unconscious, and the key to this part of man seems to be with art alone, through its handling of rhythms and symbols of ancient power.

Unfortunately, the subject of the instrumental power of religious art is complicated by the ambiguous position, in this respect, of bad religious art. Religious uglinesses and senti-mentalities seriously repel some people; but to other people they do seem to be means of grace. For instance, a recent com-petition in the *Methodist Recorder* on 'Hymns that have helped me' revealed many cases of genuine spiritual change for the good wrought through verses and tunes that are sheer twaddle; Sunday School Anniversaries and constant repetition of 'All in the April e-e-evening' seem to be about the only spiritual diet that some people will accept; I even remember how myself, during one long crisis of my life, I was greatly helped by 'Count your blessings'. No doubt the good which these things do is effected not by the sentimentalities as such, but by the element of gospel truth which is also contained in them; but the gospel truth does seem to be received because of the senti-mentalities which accompany it. True, it is harder to judge what effects these things have on the other side—how many men of taste they drive away to erroneous but more gracious forms of religion, how many men they hold down on lower levels of truth and experience than those which should be aspired to, how many they lead to think that the Church deals only in puerilities and need be no concern of grown men.

The sum total of these bad effects cannot be estimated; but it must be massive. Moreover, dare we in these matters do evil that good may come? And dare we depart from the austere example of Our Lord, who never spoke a word of weak or false feeling? Yet, when we abandon the sentimentalities, then left-wing sects take them up, and with them do a work of partial good among folk to whom we could in theory do a greater good, but with whom we have lost contact.

(4) Part of what has been said above, on the intrinsic and instrumental values of art, may be put usefully in this way: *Art is a part, and a good part, of life; it therefore can and must be sanctified*. God is in all good things and claims all good things as His own; can we then properly seek to withhold art from Him?

(5) The great French critic, the Abbé Bremond, has argued most persuasively that *art and religion, when each is at its highest, do the same thing*. He equates the poetic and the mystical faculties; the deepest insights of the great poets and the deepest insights of the great saints are the same insights.

(6) The next justification for religious art blends into the higher forms of some of those presented already, but takes us higher still. *Religious art leads us into the very life of God*, and this in ways not open to any other approach.

Here we must pause to consider the nature of religious experience. 'Man's chief end is to glorify God and enjoy Him for ever'; we all agree with the Scottish Catechism on that. But *how* are we to glorify God and enjoy Him? Here again we all agree, in general terms, for Our Lord Himself has told us: we are to love God and our fellow men. Unfortunately, however, our interpretation of what it means to love God is often too narrow. We think of this love as a relationship between ourselves and another Person like ourselves but vaster. This is indeed true as far as it goes; but by itself it is far too anthropomorphic to be the whole truth. We call God our Father, rightly; we call Him the Source and Being of moral goodness, rightly; on this basis we think of 'experience' of Him and the whole range of the spiritual life as being closely like friendships within a family, and this too is right as far as it goes; but it is seriously insufficient if taken to be the whole truth about the spiritual life. The Protestant preoccupation with salvation and morality and sonship has prevented many of us from taking seriously enough the great truths enunciated by the Schoolmen—that God's Personality, though real, is 'analogical', having infinitely greater fulness than human personality, and that He has other attributes besides moral goodness. God is not only the Good Father; He is also the Source and Being of Truth and Beauty. Full experience of Him must therefore make contact with those aspects of His Being, with His more metaphysical and aesthetic Self, as in Dante's vision :

Ah, overflowing grace, by which I dared to fix my gaze so long on the eternal light that I consumed my sight in it!

In its depths I saw enclosed, bound by love in one volume, all that is scattered throughout the universe;

substance and accidents and their relations, as though fused together in such a way that what I speak of is one single flame.

Accordingly, the full communion with God, to correspond to the full Nature of God and apprehend His attributes of Truth and Beauty, must include science and art. These are not distractions from God Himself, nor are they optional extras for those with tastes that way and a special right to that kind of relaxation; they are, as much as what is commonly called 'religious experience', parts of the great quest towards the One Universal Goal.

(7) *Religious art can be a proper offering to God*. This further element in my justification of religious art I bring forward with hesitation, since I am myself far from clear as to what it means. It does somehow seem true that we men feel that, 'although we be unworthy, through our manifold sins, to offer unto' God 'any sacrifice', yet sacrifice we must; we must needs offer of our best to God; and this has often been taken to include our offering to God some costly beauty. The descriptions of the Tabernacle and the Temple, and many passages of the Psalms, imply this feeling in the Old Testament; and Our

Lord explicitly accepts it for Himself (though perhaps as a unique case) in the episode of the woman with the alabaster box of ointment. In the spirit of this is Wordsworth's sonnet in justification of King's College Chapel, 'Tax not the royal Saint with vain expense'. The concept of offering to God bristles with difficulties which I cannot myself see through; but neither can I ignore the great body of testimony from donors and artists, that, when they have given to God the finest art that they could, they were sure that such was the right thing to do and that their offering was accepted and blessed.

BOOKS RECOMMENDED

Apart from Geddes MacGregor: *Aesthetic Experience in Religion*, there seems to be no full-sized general book, written originally in English, on this most important subject, and I do not myself find Dr. MacGregor's book helpful except on occasional points. Paul Tillich: *Theology of Culture*, might help those who, unlike myself, find Dr. Tillich intelligible. There is good matter, though inevitably it is not fully organized, in the symposium on 'Christianity and the Arts' in the July 1958 number of *The London Quarterly and Holborn Review*, pp. 161–86; and in *The Student World*, No. 2, 1955 (W.S.C.F., Geneva), 'Faith, Art and Culture'; and in Bro. George Every: *Christian Discrimination*. (The symposium, *The Church and the Arts*, ed. Frank Glendenning (S.C.M.), was unfortunately published too late for me to be able to use it in the preparation of this booklet. It is short, and suffers from some of the usual defects of composite authorship; but it is full of good things, and I most heartily recommend its reading.) A. G. Hebert: *Liturgy and Society*, still has value.

There is much good literature on the subject in French. Note especially:

H. Bremond: *Prière et poésie* (Out of print. An Eng. trans., *Prayer and Poetry*, also out of print, can be borrowed at or through libraries.)

P.-R. Régamey, O.P.: *Art sacré au XXe siècle?* (An English trans. is in preparation.)

Yves Sjöberg: *Mort et résurrection de l'art sacré*

On special points, the following are valuable:

W. R. Lethaby: *Architecture, Nature, and Magic*

W. A. Visser 't Hooft: *Rembrandt and the Gospel* (Eng. trans.)

25

QUESTIONS FOR DISCUSSION

1. Which of the following statements is true? (*a*) All honest work in art is religious. (*b*) The subject makes a difference. If (*b*), what difference?

2. How are your prayers affected by: (*a*) a church, (*b*) its music, (*c*) Bach heard in a concert hall, (*d*) Bach heard on a gramophone, (*e*) Gounod's '*Ave Maria*', (*f*) using words such as those of the Collect for the Fourth Sunday after Trinity (see p. 47)?

3. What ought to be done about Sunday School Anniversaries, and why?

4. In which of these types of fellowship can you worship (*a*) most easily, and (*b*) most deeply? (i) A Quaker Meeting, (ii) a Salvation Army meeting in the barracks, (iii) a Methodist prayer-meeting, (iv) a Presbyterian Sunday morning Service, (v) Anglican 'Low Church' Mattins, (vi) High Mass. Why? (*N.B.*: Visit any of these that you do not already know at first hand.)

5. Inscription under a stained-glass window: 'To the Glory of God and in Memory of A.B. . . .'. What do you take that to mean?

6. What do you take to be the lesson, as regards art, of Matthew 26 [6-13] (Mark 14 [3-9]; Luke 7 [36-50]; John 12 [1-8])?

THREE

How Modern Religion Should Use Art

RELIGIOUS ART is enjoying some measure of revival in modern times, and in this revival religious architecture has a long lead over the other religious arts. This is partly because architecture, owing to the stimuli peculiar to it (new techniques, opportunity for refreshing ways of team-work, the discipline imposed by the practical needs of the client), is much the most progressive and satisfactory of the modern arts, and because war-time destruction and peace-time shifts of population have recently made necessary the building of new churches—whereas 'decoration can wait'. Much of this new building has been quite lamentable, but some of it points the way to what could be one of the greatest ages of religious building.

In those cases where modern church architecture has been good, that has been because two sets of principles have been observed, the first theological, the second aesthetic.

The first, the theological, set of principles can be summed up as enjoining the subordination of church architecture to the 'liturgy', that is, to the intentions and requirements of public worship, properly understood. If we are building well now, it is partly because we are now asking, before we build, What shall we be building for? That may seem an obvious thing to do, but it is amazing how often our forefathers neglected to do it; they indulged in *a priori* notions about 'plans' and thoughtlessly copied outmoded 'styles', largely because their own idea of the 'liturgy', the task performed in public

27

worship, was so vague. Often in the past we built, or at any
rate contrived to look as if we built, for a concert, in which
now an orator, now the choir, was to take the lead, set against a
background, highly suitable in that context, of organ-pipes. We
are now trying to create buildings which will adequately house
and symbolize all that is meant by a gathering of the local
family of God to hear the Word and receive the Sacraments.
In the church itself, so far as new buildings are concerned, we
are doing away with a choir behind the preacher, a Lord's
Table dwarfed by the pulpit, a congregation split in two between ground floor and gallery, a tiny cramped 'sanctuary'
within which the minister can scarcely move, and a font which
is a little portable jar set on the Lord's Table and overshadowed
by the peonies. We are rejecting these things not because they
are ugly—indeed, they never *need* be ugly, and often *are* not—
but because they do not express and forward the spiritual
reality of our gatherings, our liturgical purpose, which is to
be the local family of God in reception of Word and Sacraments. Our ancillary buildings—vestries, crush hall, kitchen,
cloakrooms and the like—though not so directly amenable to
theological criticism, can be and should be so designed as to
subserve, worthily and happily, the main purpose of the
church.

The second set of principles is aesthetic; they can be summed
up as honesty and adventure with modern materials. Rein-
forced concrete, new kinds of glass and new ways with glass,
new paints, fabrics, systems of heating, of lighting, of seating,
of ventilation—all these unite to give exciting new opportunities in church building, and only foolish or unduly sentimental
people mistrust them. I have called the acceptance of them
a matter of *aesthetic* principle, and so in the main it is—it is a
matter for judgement by taste, and for guidance by the man
with the technical expertness; and those responsible for getting
a new church built generally do well to leave aesthetic questions to the architect, if he is a good one, instead of confusing
things with their amateurish likes and dislikes. Nevertheless,
this principle has its *religious* side also. Surely honesty, adven-

ture, relevance to the modern world, are virtues of spiritual importance. It is not merely a technical matter, but mainly a spiritual matter, that we should aim at appearing to our neighbourhoods to be not sentimental fuddy-duddies but men with a message for the times.

If these two sets of principles are honoured, then architect and client together will be well on the way to providing a worthy church. It will have no ugliness, no sentimentality; it will have some measure of positive beauty—this will vary with the architect's ability and other circumstances.

Is that all there is to be aimed at in a church? No; there ought to be also that special quality ƒ 'numinousness', of holding the Presence, which is easier felt than defined. A building for worship ought to have about it that mysterious something which inspires worship as mere beauty does not.

I am personally inclined to think that the very greatest religious architecture goes beyond even that, and not only is able to lead a congregation to worship, but itself worships. I think that sub-human Nature can and does worship God—that the *Benedicite* and the *Cantemus cuncti* are meant literally—because His praise is what God made Nature for; and in favoured times and places I think I can feel parts of Nature engaged on this worship. It may then be that man at his greatest can share even in this highest aspect of the work of creation. He can, like God, mould things to forms of beauty; may he not at times mould them even to forms of worship? Certainly in some buildings, in some circumstances, I feel that the building is actually speaking the Divine praise. Perhaps, put thus, this is false mysticism, sentimental and dishonest thinking on my part; but at least it points to a fact, that in the greatest religious architecture the power to lead the soul to worship reaches transcendent heights.

It may be that these rarities are beyond us at our present stage. It may be that they need a larger scale than that on which we usually build. It may be also that ferro-concrete styles, which would seem to be the only honest styles for large-scale building today, still need to achieve more maturity in

29

religious use, more shedding of the strident secular values in whose service they were first evolved: and we need much more experiment towards what will be an honest style, in a ferro-concrete age, for those smaller buildings in which ferro-concrete would be an unwieldy material and ferro-concrete styles would be incongruous. Above all we need, if we are to reach the heights, a more solid community sense of religion than we have now; we need to have congregation, outer world, architect and builders all united in one socially-held faith. But it may be that God will permit this generation to begin to make the tradition in which later the heights will be scaled.

So much for architecture. What of the other visual arts? With them, I think, we can only go slowly for the time being. Modern architecture eschews much decoration, and is only just learning how to be happy in incorporating fresco and sculpture and good coloured glass. Architecture has greatly needed the present urge towards simple and honest reliance on the grace and mass of mere structural line and material; the pendulum may have swung too far in that direction, but its return to the centre cannot well be hurried. Besides, can we trust our people yet in these matters? Decorations tend to be brought in after the architect has lost control of the building; so, if once we let the idea get abroad that we should be glad to receive ornaments beyond what are essential and incorporated in the design, all sorts of nonsense may be thrust upon us. It is hard to refuse well-meant donations, particularly when they are offered, as they so often are, in memory of the dead. So, unless circumstances are really propitious, let us insist on a sanctified plainness.

BOOKS RECOMMENDED

Convenient small books on modern trends, well-illustrated, are:
  Sir Edward Maufe: *Modern Church Architecture*
  Edward D. Mills: *The Modern Church*
  Incorporated Church Building Society: *Fifty Modern Churches* and *Sixty Post-War Churches*

Anton Henze and Theodor Filthaut: *Contemporary Church Art*, is larger and more expensive, and covers the 'minor arts' as well as architecture. Peter Hammond: *Liturgy and Architecture*, is full on the theological side and has a large bibliography. Gilbert Cope: *Symbolism in the Bible and the Church*, vii, conveniently summarizes the same general line of thought. Peter F. Anson: *Fashions in Church Furnishings: 1840–1940*, is encyclopaedic within its range. For many years a wider set of church adornments has been under useful criticism in the successive editions of Percy Dearmer: *The Parson's Handbook*. As regards music, see Erik Routley: *Church Music and Theology*. A. C. Bridge: *Images of God*, is useful, though in some ways strange. An invaluable American pamphlet, *Documents for Sacred Architecture*, by Cardinal Lercaro and the Roman Catholic bishops of Germany, is available from Duckett's of the Strand for 1s. 3d. plus postage.

For keeping abreast of so rapidly changing a situation, periodicals are in some ways more useful than books. *Art d'église* (Abbaye de Saint-André, Bruges), *L'art sacré* (Éditions du Cerf, Paris), *Liturgical Arts* (New York) and *Church Buildings Today* (John Catt, Downham, Billericay), are specially helpful. Much useful material appears in the illustrated Annual Reports of the Central Council for Churches, published every few years (and notably in the 1960 number, *Both Old and New*), in the illustrated Annual Reports of the Methodist Church's Department for Chapel Affairs, in the cyclostyled occasional bulletins of the New Churches Research Group and in the newsletters of the Society of Christian Artists.

QUESTIONS FOR DISCUSSION

1. What improvements are needed in your church building for the most helpful conduct of (*a*) the Sacrament of Holy Communion, (*b*) the Sacrament of Baptism, (*c*) ordinary public worship, (*d*) weddings, and (*e*) the participation by children in public worship? (*N.B.*: The same building will have to serve for all these purposes.)

2. What is right and what is wrong with (*a*) a 'Gothic' church, (*b*) a 'Brunswick'-style church, (*c*) a 'dual-purpose hall'?

3. You will have heard it said: 'I like a church to *look* like a church.' What does this generally mean? What, if anything, *ought* it to mean?

4. If you could replace your present church by a new one, how would you instruct the architect? (Assume, what is never the case

in real life, that you have both reasonable funds and dictatorial powers.)

5. Ought (*a*) the pulpit, (*b*) the Lord's Table, (*c*) anything else, be that towards which a church's architecture primarily draws the eye?

6. You would like to have a new church, but you have inherited an 'old horror', and will have to put up with it. How would you set about improving it, if you had £3,000 to spend and no one's feelings but your own to take account of? (*N.B.*: You will do right to think of big schemes of carpentry and re-painting; but don't disdain also to remember the mess in the forecourt, the junk on top of the vestry cupboard, the leaning, faded notice-board, and the poster which still urges attendance at last December's pea-and-pie supper.)

7. Your church has no structural needs. Its Trust has received £100 'for the erection within the church of a suitable memorial to A.B.' How would you advise that the money be spent?

8. How would you seek to reform certain commercial 'Church Art Furnishers'? (*N.B.*: Remember the law against violence.)

9. How would you draft a polite letter to Miss Smith-Jones, declining her kind offer, for the Preachers' Vestry, out of the effects of her late Aunt Emily, of an oleograph of 'Rebekah at the Well'?

10. 'The caretaker says he can't . . .' How can you help in this situation?

11. What sort of music, if any, ought to be played in church as 'voluntaries', and sung in church as 'anthems'? Why?

FOUR

Why Religion Must Suspect Art

So FAR in this booklet I have taken rather a high line with the Philistines who neglect church art or impose bad art upon the Church: and I think I have done so rightly, for their attitude is ignorant and complacent. The reply to them is in the fact of and the reasons for that long tradition in the best life of religion which has deliberately and intelligently fostered the religious use of art.

Yet it would be both unfair and unprofitable not to recognize how, parallel with that tradition, there has been also a rival tradition, a tradition of an equally deliberate and intelligent *avoidance* of art in the religious life, which may for convenience be called 'puritanism'. The Jewish Rechabites, the Indian *samnyāsins*, the early followers of Islam with their fierce simplicities, the Christian hermits from St. Pachomius onwards, the Cistercians, and those called 'Puritans' in the narrower, historical sense of the word—all these and others show various attempts, often sincerely and thoughtfully explained and defended, to reject art in the name of religion. The attempts have indeed never been complete or fully consistent; for instance, a long and interesting study could be made of the changes and compromises of Milton in this respect. But Puritanism forms one of the great world-forms of religious tradition; it is well worth while to examine what are the grounds for it.

I think that the grounds can be usefully analysed into four, though these are closely related, and perhaps are really the same idea seen from different view-points.

(1) Firstly, religion tends to reject art on the basis of a *value-judgement*. We can, it is argued, know God directly—or, if that is a heterodox way of putting it, since 'no man hath seen God at any time', we can know Him by the comparatively direct ways of prayer and worship; and this is our supreme bliss, or a foretaste of it. There are indeed other goods, beauty among them; but life is short and energies are limited, so can we afford to spend time and zeal on anything less than the best? Thus in all climes and ages the saints, who are the experts on the life with God, have tended to refuse all value to every type of experience except the direct sense of God's love. Thus St. Gregory, speaking of the gathering of the soul itself to itself, which is the first stage of contemplation, says : 'It never can gather itself to itself, till first it has learned to fence off from the mental eye all likenesses of images in heaven and on earth, to reject and trample underfoot whatever comes into its thinking from physical sight, hearing, smell, touch or taste, so that it can seek inwardly for itself such as it is without these things.' Michelangelo, in the spiritual stresses of his old age, declared that 'neither painting nor carving may any more give peace to the soul which has turned to that Divine Love which opened Its arms on the Cross to take us'. And our own Isaac Watts wrote :

> *Dead be my heart to all below,*
> *To mortal joys and mortal cares:*
> *To sensual bliss that charms me so*
> *Be dark, my eyes, and deaf, my ears.*

Such thinkers have, for the most part, though not invariably, felt constrained to allow some place in life for the pursuit of moral values, and sometimes also a limited place for the pursuit of beauty, regarded strictly as a moral and religious instrument; but they deny beauty any final value, not indeed in itself, but in comparison with the higher goods of religion and of

34

character which could be apprehended in the same time and with the same spiritual energy.

Nevertheless, we ought to remember that this same kind of judgement, if carried out relentlessly, will bring bad art under a very heavy condemnation, since ugliness and sentimentality are not mere absences of beauty and integrity, but are actual dis-values. If, then, by an inescapable value-judgement the ugly must be eschewed, and yet objects and sights and sounds cannot be altogether avoided, some art of a tolerable kind will have to be made and used, to avoid the sin of deliberate use of the bad.

(2) Religion also tends to reject art by a *moral judgement*. I mean by this, that only two values in human life carry an unmistakable 'ought' with them, and art is not one of those two. Everyone knows that he *ought* to be good; everyone who believes in God knows that he *ought* to seek experience of Him; but can we in the same way say of anyone that he *ought* to pursue art? This is a vague question: it would mean rather different things when applied to different people, or even to the same people at different times. It might have one meaning and one answer when applied to a professional artist in his working hours, and others to the same man on his 'day off'; others to an average housewife while busy with her children; others to the same woman when choosing her wallpaper; others to a desert hermit; others to a sixth-former choosing his career. But I doubt if in any case we are as definite in our moral judgements about artistic matters as we are upon matters called 'moral' in the sense of concerned with inter-personal action. Probably we would say that a true artist *ought* not to stoop to pot-boiling, at any rate for his own profit, and that an educated man, in normal circumstances, *ought* to give some place in his life to culture; but moral judgements like those seem to be of a weaker and more guarded kind than that which says of an artist or of an educated man or of any other human being that he *ought* if possible to avoid hurting children. Art's claim would never seem to be as strong as a purely moral claim; for instance, the Parthenon was built with stolen money, and, if

that was the only way in which it could have been built, it ought not to have been built. Even when there is not such a clear clash of standards as that, yet art seems morally to be a mere optional; and in a crowded life ought anyone of spiritual zeal to spend time and energy on a mere optional, when his love of God and his moral character still need so much betterment? '*Honte à qui peut chanter pendant que Rome brûle*': 'Shame on one who can sing while Rome is afire.'

Yet that austere question and that puritan judgement may not present the only relevant outlook. The judgement, after all, is expressed in a line of poetry, which hardly seems consistent with a denial of art's right to exist! There are four factors to consider on the other side. In the first place, we must not forget the instrumental value of art in forwarding moral and religious ends. Secondly, we must recall a point already made, that art of some kind is inevitable whenever we make anything, including even sentences of speech. Thirdly, there are some moral questions, and this may be one of them, to which there is no universal answer for all men, but only separate answers for each separate person according to his own individual abilities, temperament and circumstances. Fourthly, may not the fact of the extreme badness of bad art again in some measure come to our rescue here? For, even if there is no strong moral case for the promotion of good art, is there not a very strong moral case for the avoidance of bad art? Acquiescence in standards which are low and, on some interpretations of them, are actually dishonest, is, in the case at any rate of those who are better instructed, a moral fault of some seriousness; it may even come perilously close to the ultimate sin of calling evil good.

(3) Religion tends to reject art by a *pastoral judgement*. This is essentially the same rejection as the last, put in the way that comes naturally to us in the Church who feel responsibility for furthering Christian fellowship. To us it seems self-evident that prayerful men of simple mind and heart, uneducated men of kindness and spirituality, are men as good as the greatest geniuses with the same spiritual powers; we simply do not find

36

it necessary or right to judge of them that they would be 'better men' if they also cultivated a better taste in music—or, if we do, it is only in a very moderate and hesitating way. At almost all costs we must, for love's sake and the Church's sake and our own souls' sake, keep open full spiritual communion with them; yet this may require us to join heartily in poor music and to acquiesce in sentimental building schemes. We feel it our pastoral duty also to keep open as full access as we can to those both inside and outside the Church who are not so fine spiritually as the 'saints', but for whose souls also we have responsibility, who will be turned away from the hearing of the Gospel if we deny them their sentimentalities and bad art, or if we become, or become thought of as, a 'highbrow' clique. To put it bluntly in an illustration: We know that in many places, if the Sunday School Anniversary in its debased form were abolished, many people would lose all their scanty contact with the Church; if, therefore, I decline to stand for my artistic principles when Anniversaries in my churches are arranged, it may not be because I am frightened of decreased collections and offended teachers, but because I have a genuine Christian concern for those we call the 'casuals', and am unwilling to lose contact with them. Simplicity and love are essential Christian virtues; if they are not set in the very forefront of our intent, any stand for aesthetic values easily becomes intellectual snobbery, as is clearly shown in Aristotle's '*megalopsychos*' and '*megaloprepēs*' (the 'proud' man and the 'magnificent' man), whom antiquity's greatest thinker but one took to be the fine flowers of his culture, and whom we Christians now know to be close relatives of the Devil.

Some of the finest spirits of our time find this pastoral concern taking them very far along an anti-cultural road. Somewhat as many godly men, like St. Francis, loving their brethren in economic need, have been impelled by that love to give up all their money, and therewith many cultural opportunities, so in this age, in which economic poverty is much less rampant but the cultural divisions of society are becoming tragically deep, some feel an inner call to give up their culture also, with a Franciscan love and with the reward of a Franciscan joy. One cannot help people unless one stands where they stand. Hence I know of one famous youth-club leader who, while taming an adolescent gang, used to hide with them from the police. I met recently a cultivated young lady who for the sake of her youth club was deliberately spending her evenings listening to and learning to enjoy 'pop-songs' and similar entertainments, because unless she did so she could not join naturally in the club conversations. Can we have friendly contacts with the ordinary folk of our generation unless we can talk knowledgeably and sympathetically about such things; and are not such contacts an overriding obligation upon us? Surely the Gospel is not for the grammar-school product only, but for the secondary-modern-school product as well; and how can we win him if we cannot talk his language?

And yet there is so much to be said on the other side. How far dare we do evil that good may come? If we deny our own known standards, do we remain the kind of people who can really help anyone? There are indeed certain spiritual risks that all active Christians have to take, but how far dare we trifle with our own souls' integrity? How far can we thus trifle, and yet pray God to 'lead us not into temptation'? And, if we drag down standards to help some, what of others who will see this, and then will reject a Gospel which has been unworthily presented? What have we to give, if we have slighted our sense of reverence?

(4) Christianity tends to reject art also by a *Biblical judgement*. This is the same rejection as the others, put now in terms of authority. The Bible's teaching on how to live puts almost exclusive stress on moral character and the love of God : 'What doth the Lord require of thee, but to do justly, and to love mercy, and to walk humbly with thy God?' There is no explicit polemic against art as such (only against certain forms of it associated with idolatry, luxury or social callousness); but there is such a general neglect of art and stress on the exclusive claims of other values that some critics have judged great tracts of the Bible to be deeply opposed to art.

38

There are indeed a few texts which can be quoted on the other side; though maybe we use them too much and use them out of their contexts. Paul exhorted us to 'think on' (or 'reckon as of advantage') 'whatsoever things are lovely', but the word translated 'lovely' refers to pleasing traits of character and personality rather than to beauty of art. More convincing are the facts that parts of the Old Testament revel in the rich adornment of the Temple and the musical praise of God; that the Book of Revelation describes the soul's eternal life with God in sparkling scenes of great richness; that the Bible as a whole is great literature (though in most parts not so fine in the originals as in our normal translations), and in particular that Jesus Himself was a consummate artist with the parable-form.

I have to some extent countered each of these four types of rejection as it was presented. It may be thought that they are countered as a whole by what was urged in the last Chapter about beauty being a part of the Nature of God, and thus necessary for a full apprehension of Him. I am not sure, however, whether that doctrine, though true, and important in its place, can in fact lead us to any firm conclusions as regards this particular problem. Before we can draw conclusions from the nature of the full apprehension of God to rules of conduct for this present life, we have first to ask : Do we, ought we to, aim at a full apprehension of God in this life? To those brought up on certain forms of the doctrine of 'experience', this may seem a strange, even a shocking, question to ask; but Christian thought at its best has always distinguished clearly between the type of experience that we can have (miracle apart) and should seek when *in via*, while still on our pilgrimage, and that which is promised for us when *in patria*, after we have reached our Heavenly Home. The classic formulation of this doctrine is in Aquinas; the essence of it was repeated by John Wesley in his polemic against William Law and the mystics; it has a firm Biblical basis in several texts like 'No man hath seen God at any time'; and it is rooted in common sense as well, since God must be presumed to know the position of every electron in the universe and the date of every least event in history and to enjoy the rainbow beauty of every crystal hidden in the earth's crust—and so one could go on and on to infinity hinting at the inconceivable riches of His knowledge of facts and of beauties. No sane person claims that his experience of God gives him access to more than the tiniest fragment of this vast store : it is clear, then, that our knowledge of God in this life is not and cannot be knowledge of His full Nature. It would seem that for us here the main appointed ways of contacting and sharing the life of God are faith, prayer, love and good conduct, and that His full Nature of Truth and Beauty, though some at least of it is to be seen by us hereafter, is not for us as yet. How far we are entitled to receive and even seek for foretastes, is another and a very delicate problem.

It is clear that what has been said in this last paragraph would minimize the place of science just as much as that of art, since knowledge is as much a part of God's nature as is beauty. But this is a line of thought which we cannot pursue here.

BOOKS RECOMMENDED

The inescapable text on life with God is Dante's *Paradiso*, and more particularly its last four cantos.

On the question of the relation of the values to God, in time and in eternity, the best thinking (after old Thomas Traherne's *Centuries of Meditations*) is that by the school of 'British Idealism' and the theologians influenced by it—now under a shadow which I am sure will only be temporary. See :

P. H. Wicksteed : *The Religion of Time and the Religion of Eternity*

F. von Hügel : *The Mystical Element of Religion* and *Eternal Life*

A. S. Pringle-Pattison : *The Idea of God*

A. E. Taylor : *The Faith of a Moralist*, I. iii, vi–ix

K. E. Kirk : *The Vision of God*

John Baillie : *And the Life Everlasting* (esp. pp. 24–27, 134, 153, 198–237)

On the general relations between culture and religion, see the Abbé Bremond's book already referred to. There is much pagan wisdom in J. C. Powys's *The Meaning of Culture*. See also Geddes

MacGregor's book already referred to, and H. Richard Niebuhr's *Christ and Culture.*

The very instructive mediaeval controversy on the place of culture in the religious life can be studied in :

Jacques Maritain : *Art and Scholasticism* (Eng. trans.)

Dom Jean Leclercq : *L'amour des lettres et le désir de Dieu.* (The Epilogue, pp. 236–250, is the finest piece of thought that I know on the relation of art to religion).

In a popular form, Helen Waddell's great novel, *Peter Abelard* (now paper-backed).

Religious suspicion of the arts is well and moderately expressed by Derek Kidner in an I.V.F. pamphlet, *The Christian and the Arts*, which has a special interest as being written from the standpoint of modern fundamentalism, which has rarely found voice in these debates.

What I have called the 'pastoral rejection' has been made, or partly made, by three great priest-poets in the course of intense spiritual agonies; and the texts which relate these deserve the most careful study. They are :

Gerard Manley Hopkins : pp. 4–6, 192–195 in the Penguin Poets edition

Thomas Merton : *Elected Silence*

R. S. Thomas : *Song at the Year's Turning*

QUESTIONS FOR DISCUSSION

1. Consider Matthew 5^{29-30}; Mark 13^{1-2}; 1 Corinthians 1^{18-31}; Philippians 3^{7-11}. What place do these leave for art in the religious life?

2. Consider Genesis 1; Exodus 35–39; Job 38–41; Psalms 104, 150; Song of Songs 4; Matthew 6^{28-29}; Philippians 4^8; Revelation 21–22^5. What place do these leave for puritanism?

3. Consider *The Methodist Hymn-Book*, Nos. 546, 563, 598. How far can you really sing them?

4. What sacrifice of our standards, if any, ought we to make for the sake of Christian fellowship with those (*a*) inside and (*b*) outside the Church?

FIVE

The Answer in a Compromise
and a Quest

I THINK it is already clear, from the way the last Chapter has developed, that there is no one definite, clear-cut, text-book answer to the problem of the place of art in the Christian life. As in most moral choices in life, we have two sets of goods confronted in dialogue, in tension; and the right answer is not found by any application of a rule, but by sensitivity to pressures on the spirit, or, in Christian terms, by the guidance of the Spirit working through our whole self when that self is well-trained and obedient.

In most cases, the answer will not be a complete victory for either side in the tension, but something which could be called, if the word is not thought too defeatist, too uncommitted, a compromise. A better word in some ways would be 'quest', as that expresses the need of an active, seeking soul; on the other hand that word does not, as 'compromise' does, indicate the fact that for most of us the answer will be found somewhere between two extremes. If we were fully saved souls, we should be able effortlessly and continually to see all things in God, and no problem would arise for us. As we are, we need both to seek that God who is above all His creatures, by His main appointed ways of faith, prayer, service and love; and we need also, so far as we can, to see the richness of His Being in knowledge and beauty, and to receive the aid which He graciously gives us through His Self-revelation in the experiences of science and of art.

Thus most of us will find that we need, for our maximum development and service, to use all our powers in turn. What Professor W. E. Hocking in a slightly different context called 'the principle of alternation' applies here: we cannot maintain any one type of spiritual activity for long, yet we need never 'cease' altogether 'from mental strife', except in sleep; we can just turn from one type of activity to another, and thus rest and exercise each of our potentialities in turn. In this way direct religious experience, secular beauty, religious art and other types of high activity can normally have each its place in life—though for people of certain temperaments and in certain circumstances a more ascetic line may be the right one as regards beauty, as it may be as regards other powers (Matthew 19 [12]).

Compromise, or quest, is thus in general the way; but no one can state any definite rules for it. The problems involved are highly personal, and can only be solved each by a separate intuition. People's gifts and circumstances differ so much that no one can draw up a blue-print for universal application, or even expound any set of general principles according to which individuals are to work out their own salvations for themselves. This quest is indeed a large part of what is known as 'making oneself', and that in the last resort must be each person's own responsibility and planning. No doubt educationists in various guises—not only teachers, but also parents, parsons, writers—can help in some vague ways; but in the last resort only Dr. Bronowski can decide on whether he ought to be expert in poetry as well as in science, only Le Corbusier on whether he shall paint as well as build, only Michelangelo on whether he is to write sonnets as well as to carve, and whether at the end only prayer is really to satisfy. So for us the quest is individual. There are no rules to tell us how to divide our spare time between the National Gallery and the youth club leadership, or at what point loyalty to standards will become intellectual snobbery; the answer will vary from person to person, and will be found not in a code but in an open and dedicated heart.

In one sense, then, the quest is as individual as anything could

44

well be; but in other ways individualism in it must be sternly controlled. In the first place, both the goal and the way are not made by us, but appointed for us. We are not engaged on the humanistic mirage-hunt of 'self-development' in any mode of our own preferring, but on the religious quest of being made in the fuller likeness of God, and by a way which, though personal to us, is not of our choosing but of God's revealing.

In the second place this quest, like almost everything else for the Christian, is a thing to be attempted not in isolation, but in fellowships—in one sort of fellowship with the rest of the Church, and in another sort of fellowship with the surrounding world. All fellowship costs something; and in this fragmented age some kinds of Christian fellowship are very costly. But in these matters we *must* have fellowship, or else we are straying from the True God who is in one sense the Father of all men, into some idolatry of our own devising. Even our most personal choices about beauty will be the choices of men who are seeking to live helpfully with brethren. Many of our choices about beauty will be social choices. Only public authority backed by public opinion can decide how much public money shall be spent on proper city design. Good music and good architecture can indeed be imposed upon churches, but the fellowship is maimed if this is so, and a decision for Charles Wesley and the tunes that go with his verses rather than Sankey and the words that go with his tunes, or for a clean modern design instead of pseudo-Gothic fussiness, has not the full quality of a true act of the Church in worship until such a decision has been approved by the group-mind of the local Church as a whole.

Neither for an individual nor for a secular society nor for a Church can any clear rules for the quest be given; and no man and no society ever comes in this life to final perfection, but each solution is the starting-point of a new problem. There is thus no final answer to any part of the quest. There will always be tensions between various claims made upon us by competing values. Religious art will never quite know what or why it is, and the man of religion will never know quite how to take or to renounce his art. But there is nothing to outrage or alarm the Christian in such a situation. We have been promised a pilgrimage now, a City hereafter.

Our discussion, therefore, has led to no final answer about anything which it set out to deal with. But I hope that at least one thing has been made clear—the importance of the subject. Religious art is not the esoteric hobby of an eccentric clique. It is bound up with two matters which are of the highest concern to every Christian—the nature of the true life of the soul with God, and the mode in which the Christian faith is to be communicated. Unless we have sound judgement on the relations between religion and art, we may wander from our appointed way to the True God, and we may fail to do our appointed service of mediating His Gospel to others of His children. We need, then, for this problem the clearest and deepest thought that we can give, and the utmost grace that God can give.

QUESTIONS FOR DISCUSSION

1. What could Picasso teach the Little Puddlington Women's Bright Hour?

2. What could the Little Puddlington Women's Bright Hour teach Picasso?

3. What is the relevance of 1 Corinthians 14 to the problems that arise about our church buildings and music?

4. Was it worth while building Coventry Cathedral when most of (a) the workmen engaged on it, and (b) the citizens of Coventry, are not committed Christians?

5. Can any art or any spiritual life be fully healthy in these disordered days?

6. How can I find God's leading for me in these matters?

THE COLLECT FOR THE FOURTH SUNDAY AFTER TRINITY

O GOD, the protector of all that trust in Thee, without whom nothing is strong, nothing is holy : Increase and multiply upon us Thy mercy; that, Thou being our ruler and guide, we may so pass through things temporal, that we finally lose not the things eternal : Grant this, O heavenly Father, for Jesus Christ's sake our Lord. *Amen.*

www.ingramcontent.com/pod-product-compliance
Lightning Source LLC
Chambersburg PA
CBHW061757040426
42447CB00011B/2341